EL DINERO
MONEY

This book provides bilingual materials to teach a fun and comprehensive unit about MONEY. Included is a teacher's instruction section with details for each project along with ideas to use throughout the classroom. Discover MONEY using skills in reading, math, and spelling. Both Spanish and English versions of each project are included in one book!

Cover Photos:

Photo www.comstock.com

© 1995 PhotoDisc Incorporated

ISBN 1-59441-398-3

Dear Family Letter (pages 6–7)

Dear Family,

We are starting a unit about money. We will learn about bills, coins, and many other things relating to money.

Please join us by including money games, lessons, or discussions at home.

Family discussions will help reinforce the concepts we are learning in class.

Sincerely,

I'm on the one dollar bill.

I'm on the five dollar bill.

Send this note home with students to let families know what is happening in the classroom. The letter introduces families to the upcoming unit about money.

Money Certificate (pages 8–9)

This is a great way to recognize and reward students as they progress through the Money unit.

Use the Money Certificate as an incentive when students finish a defined list of projects or as a general award when the unit is complete. The certificates make a great classroom bulletin board display and provide students with take-home diplomas that they can be proud of.

MONEY

CERTIFICATE

Name:_____

Congratulations!
You are on your way
to a prosperous life
by learning the value
of money!

I Know My MONEY!

Copy the certificates onto colorful paper or let students color their own certificates as a classroom art project.

Money Manipulatives
(pages 10–23)

The bill and coin manipulatives included in this book can be used in a variety of ways to create fun and interesting learning games.

FLASH CARDS

Use back-to-back bills for early learners and create cards featuring different combinations of bills and coins for more advanced students. Money cards can also be mixed and matched with receipts, price tags, and checks (pages 26–29). Make several "decks" of varying difficulty to use as assessment tools.

ASSEMBLY INSTRUCTIONS

Copy the desired money manipulatives onto sturdy paper and cut them out. Laminate the manipulatives for permanent use in the classroom or make sets for each student to take home.

CONCENTRATION

This ever-popular game helps children develop memory and matching skills. Concentration works best when played in small groups.

There are several variations of "Money Concentration." Increase difficulty by mixing and matching combinations. Younger students can match bill fronts to bill backs. Advance difficulty by mixing and matching combinations. For example, have students match a card with a one dollar bill to a card with four quarters. Use checks and price tags for a more advanced game.

Price Tag
$ 1.16

ASSEMBLY INSTRUCTIONS

Copy the desired money cards onto sturdy paper and cut out. Laminate cards for permanent use.

HOW TO PLAY
1. Mix up the cards and place them facedown in rows.
2. Have students take turns choosing two cards at a time. If a student chooses two cards that match, she takes another turn. If there is no match, the next player takes a turn. The player with the most matched pairs wins the game!

Money Mobiles

This fun art project reinforces the skills and vocabulary learned in the Money unit. Use it as a classroom decoration or to identify centers that focus on different types of money.

ASSEMBLY INSTRUCTIONS

Provide crayons, paint, or markers and have students color their mobile pieces. Let them tape string, yarn, fishing line, or dental floss to the backs of the cards. Then, have them glue the coordinating cards together. When the glue dries, let them tie the cards to the header pieces. Hang the mobiles from the ceiling or in a window.

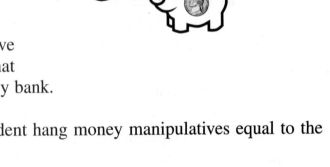

There are several options for making money mobiles:

- Give students coin manipulatives and glue. Have each student use a large piggy bank pattern (page 24) as the mobile header and write an amount of money on it. Have students find coin manipulatives that equal the amount written. Let them attach the coins to smaller piggy bank patterns (page 25).

- Glue coins to cover a large piggy bank pattern. Have a student find dollar and coin manipulatives that equal the amount of coins used to cover each piggy bank.

- Write a check as a mobile header. Have each student hang money manipulatives equal to the check amount.

- Use any combination of money manipulatives to create an interesting, fun art project that reinforces the skills and vocabulary learned in the money unit!

Writing Checks (pages 28–29)

Use blank checks to teach students how to write their own checks. Display transparencies to discuss various features of checks and give students their own blank checks to fill out during the discussion.

My Money Book (pages 30–33)

Use the covers provided (pages 30–31) or use large bills or large checks as front and back covers.

ASSEMBLY INSTRUCTIONS

Copy one book for each student. Copy cover pages onto sturdy paper and copy inside pages onto 8 ½" x 11" (21.5 cm x 28 cm) white paper. Assemble and bind books using brass fasteners or staples.

Have students write money stories about how they would spend the amount shown on their covers or have them write facts about money. Have students share their finished books with the class.

These books make a great take-home project. Have students complete several books to create their own Money libraries! Finished books also make an excellent bulletin board display.

Food Store

Have students bring food containers and labels to class to create a "food store" in your classroom. Use price tags (pages 26–27) to mark items. Let students be customers and merchants. Use money, checks, and receipts to create various "food store" game variations. Copy the "Food Store" worksheets (pages 56–59) onto transparencies and complete this activity in conjunction with them.

Privilege Points

Use price tags to mark the "cost" of privileges throughout your classroom. At a designated time each day or throughout the day, give students "receipts" or "checks" that represent certain amounts of "money." Value should be based on students' behavior and good work habits. Students can redeem their checks or receipts during scheduled privilege periods or any time you choose. Using money manipulatives for privileges makes a great incentive and helps reinforce the vocabulary and skills presented in the Money unit.

Estimada familia,

   Estamos comenzando una unidad sobre el dinero. Estamos aprendiendo sobre los billetes, las monedas y muchas cosas relacionadas con el dinero.

   Necesitamos su apoyo en la casa, incluyendo conversaciones sobre el dinero.

   Las conversaciones familiares ayudarán a fortalecer los conceptos que se aprenden en clase.

Atentamente,

Dear Family,

We are starting a unit about money. We will learn about bills, coins, and many other things relating to money.

Please join us by including money games, lessons, or discussions at home.

Family discussions will help reinforce the concepts we are learning in class.

Sincerely,

EL DINERO

CERTIFICADO

¡Conozco el valor del DINERO!

Nombre: _____

¡Felicidades!
Has comenzado una vida próspera al aprender el valor de dinero.

MONEY

CERTIFICATE

Name: _____

I Know the Value of MONEY!

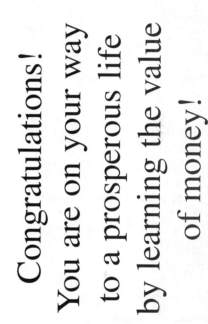

Congratulations!
You are on your way
to a prosperous life
by learning the value
of money!

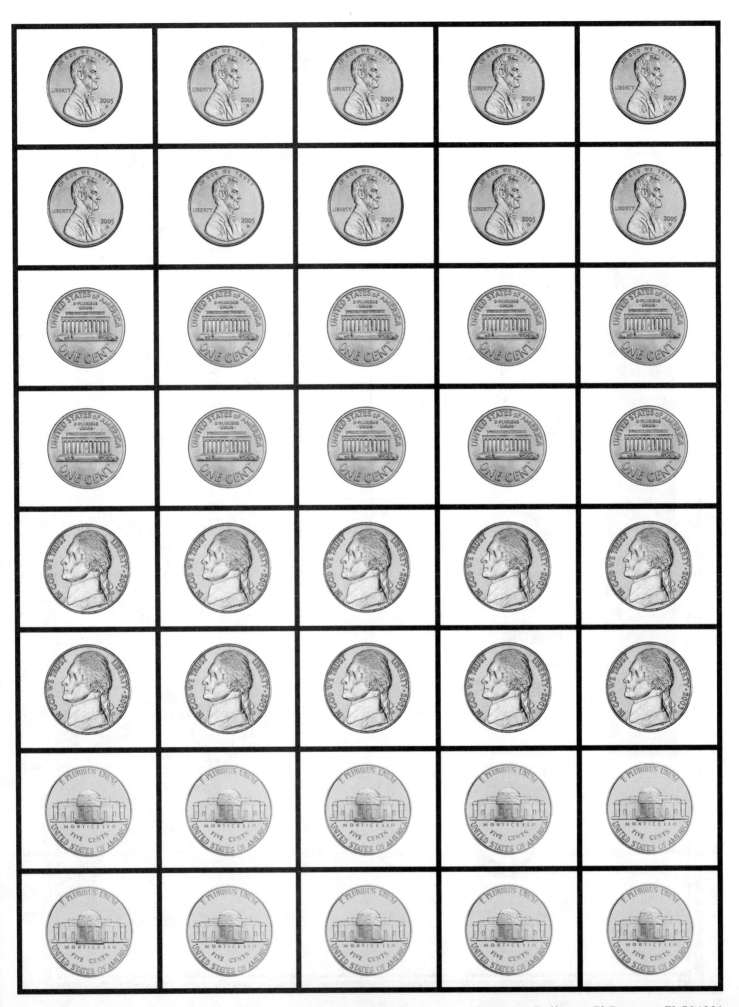

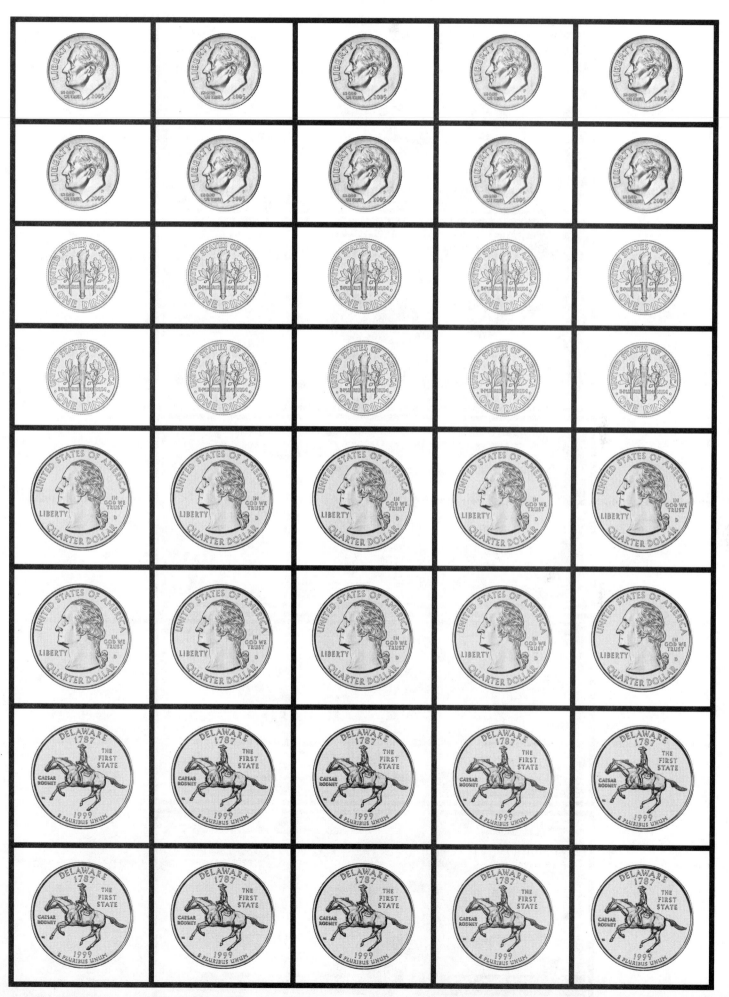

13

14

18

20 © Carson-Dellosa

22

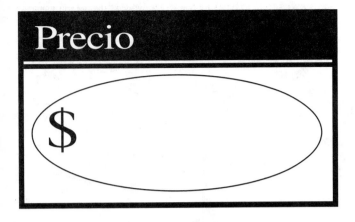

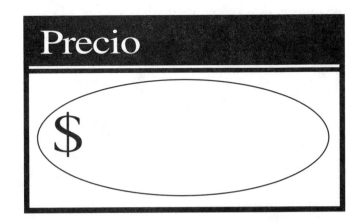

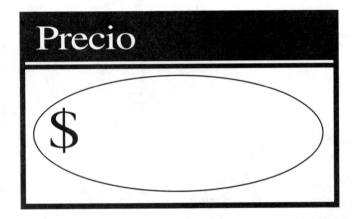

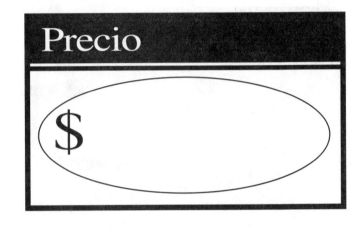

Recibo

Número de Orden: _____ Fecha: _____

Nombre:

Dirección:

Ciudad, Estado, Código postal

Vendido Por:	Efectivo	ECR	Tarjeta de Credito	En Cuenta

Cantidad	Descripción	Precio	Cantidad
		Total	

Por favor mantenga su recibo.

Recibo

Número de Orden: _____ Fecha: _____

Nombre:

Dirección:

Ciudad, Estado, Código postal

Vendido Por:	Efectivo	ECR	Tarjeta de Credito	En Cuenta

Cantidad	Descripción	Precio	Cantidad
		Total	

Por favor mantenga su recibo.

Price Tag

$

Price Tag

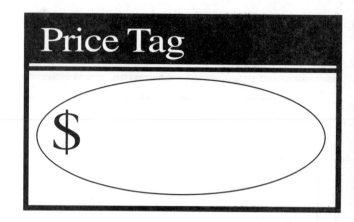

$

Price Tag

$

Price Tag

$

Receipt

Order Number: _____ Date: _____

Customer Name:

Address:

City, State, Zip Code

Sold By:	Cash	COD	Charge	On Acct.

Quantity	Description	Price	Amount
		Total	

Please keep this slip for your reference.

Receipt

Order Number: _____ Date: _____

Customer Name:

Address:

City, State, Zip Code

Sold By:	Cash	COD	Charge	On Acct.

Quantity	Description	Price	Amount
		Total	

Please keep this slip for your reference.

7777

90-1111
3333

_____ 20 _____

Pagar a la
orden de _____ $ _____

_____ Dólares

Banco de Niños

Para: _____   _____

0000555 222333333 33222222

7777

90-1111
3333

_____ 20 _____

Pagar a la
orden de _____ $ _____

_____ Dólares

Banco de Niños

Para: _____   _____

0000555 222333333 33222222

7777

90-1111
3333

_____ 20 _____

Pay to the
Order of _____ $ _____

_____ Dollars

Bank of KIDS

Memo_____   _____

0000555 2222333333 33222222

7777

90-1111
3333

_____ 20 _____

Pay to the
Order of _____ $ _____

_____ Dollars

Bank of KIDS

Memo_____   _____

0000555 2222333333 33222222

Conozco el dinero

Este libro fue hecho por:

Nombre: _____

I Know About Money

This Book Was
Created By:

Name: _____

Nombre:_____

Haz un círculo alrededor de los "pennies."

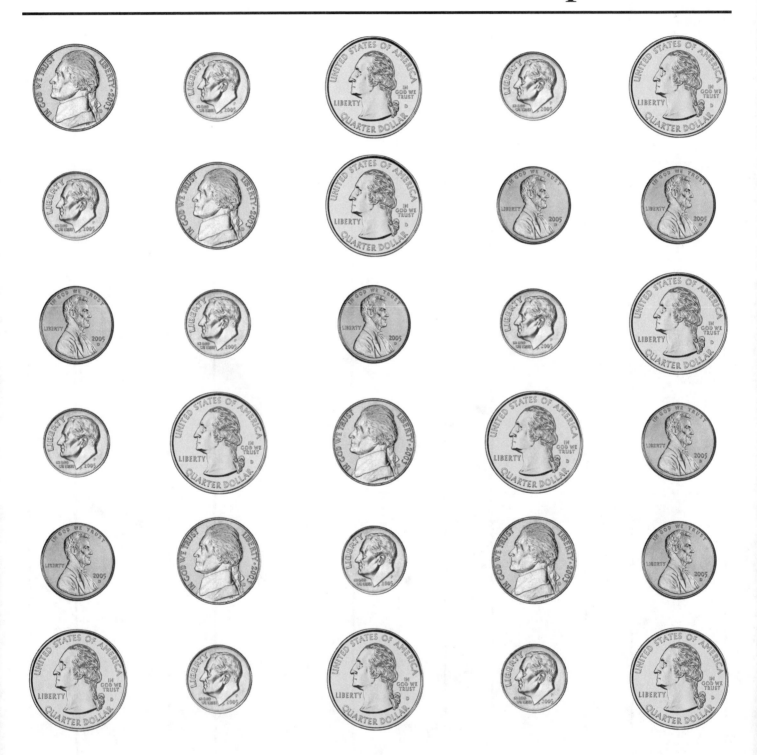

¿Cuántos círculos hiciste?_____

Circle all of the pennies.

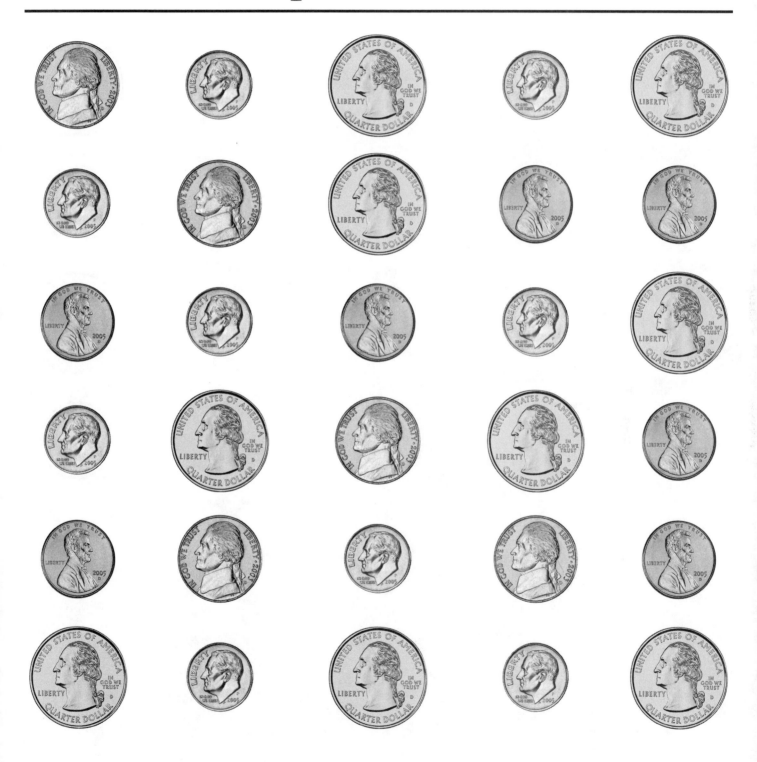

How many did you circle? _____

Haz un círculo alrededor de los "dimes."

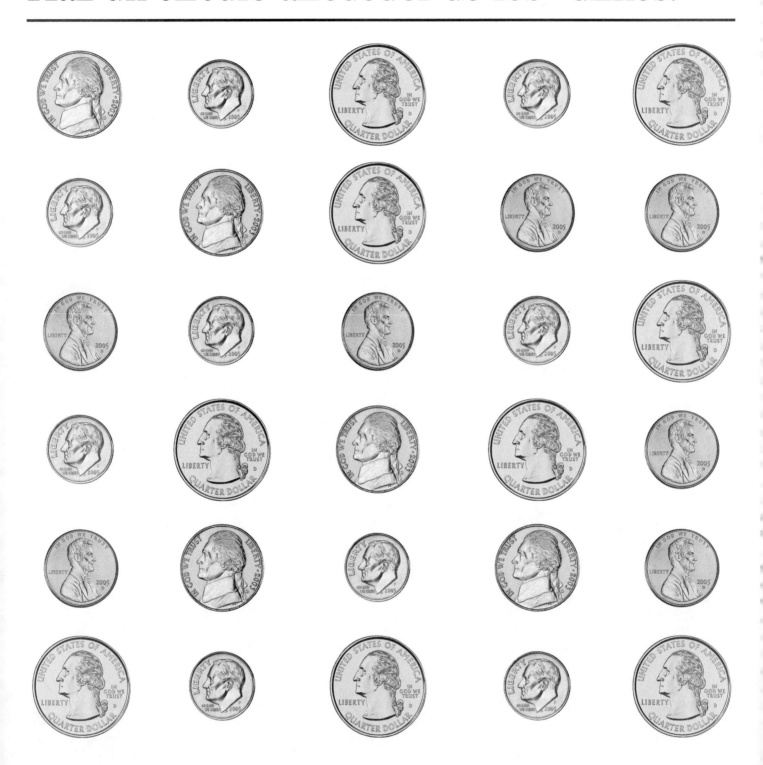

¿Cuántos círculos hiciste?_____

Name: _____

Circle all of the dimes.

How many did you circle? _____

Nombre:_____

Dibujando el "penny."

1. Mira el frente de un "penny."
   Dibuja lo que ves.

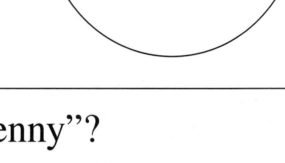

2. ¿De qué color es un "penny"?

   (Haz un círculo.)   verde   cobre   blanco

3. Mira el reverso de un "penny."
   Dibuja lo que ves.

Name:_____

Penny Draw

1. Look at the front of a penny. Draw what you see.

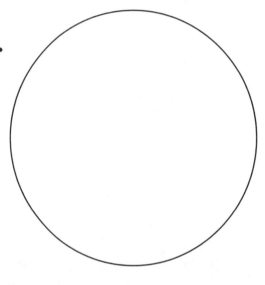

2. What color is a penny? (Circle one.)

green   copper   white

3. Look at the back of a penny. Draw what you see.

Nombre:_____

El frente de un dólar

1. Haz un círculo alrededor de la persona en el billete.
   Su nombre es George Washington. Él era un:
   (Haz un círculo.)   rey   presidente

2. ¿Cuántos números 1 puedes encontrar?

   _____

3. Haz un círculo alrededor las palabras que puedes
   encontrar que comienzan con la letra o.

4. ¿Cuántas letras 1 puedes encontrar?

   _____

Name:_____

One Dollar Bill: Front

1. Circle the man in the picture. His name is George Washington. He was a: (Circle one.)

    king   president

2. How many number 1s can you find?

_____

3. Circle the words that begin with the letter o.

4. How many letter ls can you find?

_____

Nombre:_____

El reverso de un dólar

1. Mira el reverso de un dólar.

   ¿Cuántos numeros 1 puedes encontrar? _____

2. ¿Cuántas pirámides hay? _____

3. ¿Cuántos ojos? _____

4. ¿Cuántas águilas? _____

5. ¿Cuántas palabras? _____

6. ¿Cuántas palabras comienzan con la letra o? _____

Name:_____

One Dollar Bill: Back

1. Look at the back of the dollar bill.

    How many number 1s can you find? _____

2. How many pyramids? _____

3. How many eyes? _____

4. How many eagles? _____

5. How many words? _____

6. How many words that start with the letter o? _____

Nombre:_____

Contando el dinero

Cuenta el total y completa cada problema.

1. Total: _____

   ¿Cuántos "nickels" hay?

   _____

2. Total: _____

   ¿Cuántos "pennies" hay?

   _____

3. Total: _____

   ¿Cuántos "dimes" hay?

   _____

4. Total: _____

   ¿Cuántos "quarters" hay?

   _____

5. Total: _____

   ¿Cuántos dólares hay?

   _____

Money Count

Count the total amount of money and complete each problem.

1. Total: _____

   How many nickels?

   _____

2. Total: _____

   How many pennies?

   _____

3. Total: _____

   How many dimes?

   _____

4. Total: _____

   How many quarters?

   _____

5. Total: _____

   How many dollars?

   _____

Contando el dinero

Cuenta el total.

+

$ ____

+

$ ____

+

$ ____

+

$ ____

+

$ ____

+

$ ____

+

$ ____

+

$ ____

+

$ ____

Name:_____

Money Count

Count the total amount of money.

\+

$ _____

\+

$ _____

\+

$ _____

\+

$ _____

\+

$ _____

\+

$ _____

\+

$ _____

\+

$ _____

\+

$ _____

Nombre:_____

Contando el dinero

Cuenta el total.

+

+

$ _____

$ _____

+

+

$ _____

$ _____

+

+

$ _____

$ _____

Name: _____

Money Count

Count the total amount of money.

+     +

$ _____ $ _____

+     +

$ _____ $ _____

+     +

$ _____ $ _____

Contando el dinero

Cuenta el total.

+

$

+

$

+

$

+

$

+

$

+

$

© Carson-Dellosa • El Dinero • FI-704001

Name:_____

Money Count

Count the total amount of money.

+

$ _____

$ _____

+

$ _____

$ _____

+

$ _____

$ _____

© Carson-Dellosa • Money • FI-704001

51

Nombre:_____

Contando el cochinito

Cuenta el total en
cada cochinito.

_____ ¢   _____ ¢   _____ ¢

_____ ¢   _____ ¢   _____ ¢

_____ ¢   _____ ¢   _____ ¢

Piggy Bank Count

Name:_____

Count the total amount in each piggy bank.

_____ ¢ _____ ¢ _____ ¢

_____ ¢ _____ ¢ _____ ¢

_____ ¢ _____ ¢ _____ ¢

Contando el cochinito

Cuenta el total en cada cochinito.

¢_____   ¢_____   ¢_____

¢_____   ¢_____   ¢_____

¢_____   ¢_____   ¢_____

Name:_____

Piggy Bank Count

Count the total amount in each piggy bank.

_____ ¢   _____ ¢   _____ ¢

_____ ¢   _____ ¢   _____ ¢

_____ ¢   _____ ¢   _____ ¢

Tienda de comida

$0.05 $0.10 $0.15 $0.20 $0.25 $0.30

$0.35 $0.40 $0.45 $0.50 $0.55 $0.60

1. Juan fue a la tienda. Él compró leche, 2 naranjas y 1 panecillo. Juan gastó $_____. Juan pagó con 2 billetes de un dólar. Juan recibió _____¢ de cambio. Juan gastó su cambio en 1 _____.

2. Dos niñas fueron a la tienda. Lisa compró un jugo, 2 manzanas y 1 naranja. Ana compró 1 pescado y 1 zanahoria. ¿Cúal de las 2 gastó más? _____ ¿Cuánto más gastó? _____ ¿Cuántos helados puede comprar con la diferencia? _____

3. Carlos tiene $5.00. Él compró 1 pescado, pan, maíz y 2 jugos. ¿Tiene suficiente dinero para comprar 4 tomates? _____ ¿Le darían cambio? _____ ¿Cuánto? $_____

Name:_____

Food Store

Use the values assigned below
to complete each question.

$0.05 $0.10 $0.15 $0.20 $0.25 $0.30

$0.35 $0.40 $0.45 $0.50 $0.55 $0.60

1. John went to the store. He bought milk, 2 oranges, and
    a muffin. John spent $_____. John paid with 2 one
    dollar bills. John got _____¢ back in change. John spent
    his change on 1 piece of _____.

2. Two girls went to the store. Lisa bought juice, 2
    apples, and an orange. Ann bought a fish and a carrot.
    Which girl spent more? _____ How much more did
    she spend? _____ How many ice cream cones can she
    buy with the difference? _____

3. Carl has $5.00. He bought a fish, bread, corn, and
    2 juices. Does he have enough money left to buy 4
    tomatoes? _____ Would he get change? _____
    How much? $_____

Nombre:_____

Tienda de comida

Usa las cantidades que siguen y termina cada problema.

$0.05 $0.10 $0.15 $0.20 $0.25 $0.30

$0.35 $0.40 $0.45 $0.50 $0.55 $0.60

1. Pablo tenía $1.00. Él compró _____ jugos.
   A Pablo le quedaron _____.
2. Juana gastó 85¢ y compró 1 pescado y 1 _____.
3. Susana compró 2 potes de leche y 1 panecillo y gastó
   $_____.
4. Dos niñas querían 1 caramelo y 1 naranja cada una.
   Ellas tenían $1.00 para compartir. ¿Tenían suficiente dinero?
   _____
5. Guillermo tenía $2.00 para el almuerzo. Él compró 1 pescado,
   pan y leche. ¿Cuánto cambio recibió? $_____
6. Yo compré 2 manzanas y 1 panecillo y gasté $_____.
7. El niño compró 1 tomate y 1 pan. Él tiene 90¢. ¿Cuántos
   pedazos de maíz puede comprar con su cambio? _____
8. Yo compré helado para mí y 3 amigos. Gasté $_____.
9. Marcos tenía 50¢. Él compró _____ manzanas. Le quedaron
   _____.
10. Arturo compró 2 pescados y 5 manzanas.
    ¿Cuánto gastó él? _____

Name:_____

Food Store

$0.05 $0.10 $0.15 $0.20 $0.25 $0.30

$0.35 $0.40 $0.45 $0.50 $0.55 $0.60

1. Paul had $1.00. He bought _____ juices. Paul had _____ left.

2. Jane spent 85¢ and bought a fish and a _____.

3. Susan bought 2 milks and a muffin and spent $_____.

4. Two girls each wanted a piece of candy and an orange. They had $1.00 to share. Did they have enough money?_____

5. Bill had $2.00 for lunch. He bought a fish, bread, and a milk. How much change did he get? $_____

6. I bought 2 apples and a muffin and spent $_____.

7. The boy bought a tomato and bread. He has 90¢. How many ears of corn can he buy with his change? _____

8. I bought ice cream for myself and 3 friends. I spent $_____.

9. Mark had 50¢. He bought _____ apples. He had _____ left.

10. Arthur bought 2 fish and 5 apples. How much did he spend?

    _____

Nombre:_____

Llena los espacios

 __ime

cochinit__

 __ickel

dóla__

 __enny

__onedas

Fill in the Blanks

 __ime

ban__

 __ickel

dolla__

 __enny

__oins

Llena los espacios

Escribe la letra que
falta en cada palabra.

q__arter

c__eque

dine__o

reci__o

c__mbio

pre__io

Name:_____

Fill in the Blanks

q__arter

c__eck

mon__y

recei__t

cha__ge

pri__e

Price Tag
$ 1.25

Nombre:_____

Mezcla de dinero

Haz un círculo alrededor
la cantidad correcta.

 25¢ 10¢ 1¢	 25¢ 35¢ 5¢	 11¢ 6¢ 2¢
 5¢ 25¢ 30¢	 50¢ 10¢ 20¢	 26¢ 30¢ 35¢
 35¢ 15¢ 25¢	 2¢ 10¢ 15¢	 6¢ 11¢ 14¢
 30¢ 15¢ 3¢	 30¢ 20¢ 10¢	 50¢ 10¢ 25¢

64

© Carson-Dellosa • El Dinero • FI-704001

Name:_____

Money Match

Circle the total amount of the coins shown below.

 25¢ 10¢ 1¢	 25¢ 35¢ 5¢	11¢ 6¢ 2¢
5¢ 25¢ 30¢	 50¢ 10¢ 20¢	26¢ 30¢ 35¢
35¢ 15¢ 25¢	2¢ 10¢ 15¢	6¢ 11¢ 14¢
30¢ 15¢ 3¢	30¢ 20¢ 10¢	50¢ 10¢ 25¢

Mezcla de dinero

Haz un círculo alrededor la cantidad correcta.

61¢   26¢   32¢

70¢   27¢   46¢

51¢   36¢   28¢

46¢   61¢   29¢

45¢   35¢   51¢

28¢   15¢   32¢

26¢   52¢   80¢

61¢   51¢   49¢

66

Money Match

Circle the total amount of the coins shown below.

61¢   26¢   32¢

70¢   27¢   46¢

51¢   36¢   28¢

46¢   61¢   29¢

45¢   35¢   51¢

28¢   15¢   32¢

26¢   52¢   80¢

61¢   51¢   49¢

© Carson-Dellosa • Money • FI-704001

67

Mezcla de dinero

Traza una línea desde la cantidad escrita hasta las monedas correctas.

5¢	
10¢	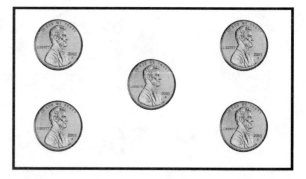
3¢	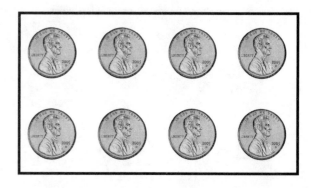
8¢	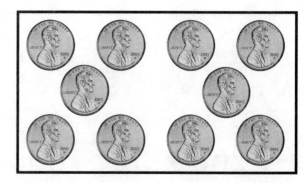

Name:_____

Money Mix

Draw a line from the money amount to the correct coins.

5¢	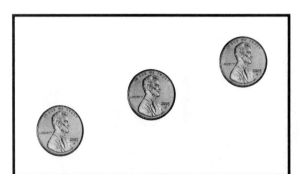
10¢	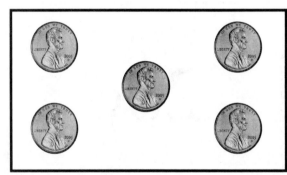
3¢	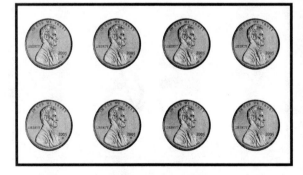
8¢	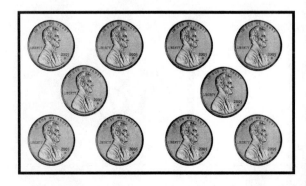

Mezcla de dinero

Traza una línea desde la cantidad
escrita hasta las monedas correctas.

10¢	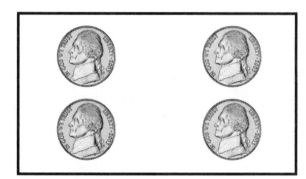
20¢	
5¢	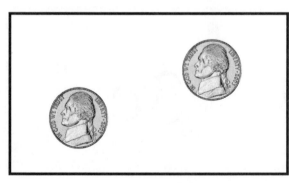
15¢	

Name:_____

Money Mix

Draw a line from the money amount to the correct coins.

10¢	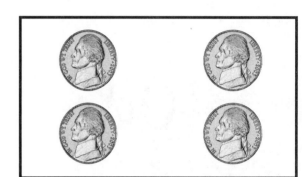
20¢	
5¢	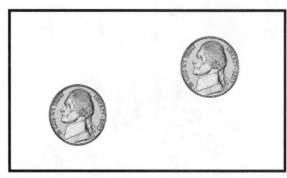
15¢	

Mezcla de dinero

Traza una línea desde la cantidad
escrita hasta las monedas correctas.

40¢	
10¢	
30¢	
60¢	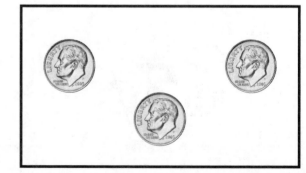

Money Mix

Draw a line from the money amount to the correct coins.

40¢	
10¢	
30¢	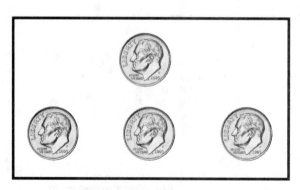
60¢	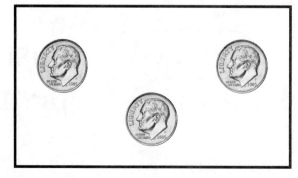

Nombre:_____

Busca las palabras

```
y  s  f  i  i  r  e  e  n  t
p  v  e  n  d  e  r  h  l  d
r  t  e  g  a  s  t  a  r  d
e  r  a (b  a  n  c  o) f  ó
c  c  w  m  e  e  t  e  d  l
i  p  e  n  n  y  o  d  s  a
o  l  t  e  i  i  t  i  o  r
h  o  p  r  y  b  e  m  e  ó
k  n  e  e  a  f  l  e  d  e
ó  b  i  l  l  e  t  e  o  s
```

(banco)   gastar   dólar   precio
dime   penny   vender billete

Word Find

Can you find the hidden words?
One word has been circled for you.
Find the other words.

```
x  b  a  n  k  s  p  e  n  d
f  k  b  i  l  l  h  e  a  c
r  c  a  s  h  c  d  e  o  o
p  a  n  n  i  n  o  o  i  s
e  i  i  s  e  l  l  m  o  t
n  x  c  c  r  h  l  f  o  h
n  o  k  r  r  c  a  b  h  a
y  d  e  t  f  e  r  u  i  s
t  n  l  s  o  l  d  y  n  p
t  d  i  m  e  m  n  o  h  t
```

bank	penny	cash	buy
dime	dollar	sell	cost
spend	sold	nickel	bill

Nombre: _____

Busca las palabras

¿Puedes encontrar las palabras escondidas?
Hicimos un círculo alrededor de "quarter."
Encuentra las otras palabras.

```
c  l  t  (q  u  a  r  t  e  r)  f  c
b  i  l  l  e  t  e  s  w  t  o  o
s  h  c  t  h  a  s  l  o  p  l  c
t  a  a  t  n  d  i  m  e  e  e  h
i  h  m  r  e  c  i  b  o  n  e  i
e  n  b  p  l  n  r  n  r  n  p  n
n  i  i  h  r  c  a  m  h  y  i  i
d  c  o  c  o  m  p  r  a  r  a  t
a  k  h  u  s  h  r  m  o  r  m  o
e  e  p  e  d  i  n  e  r  o  t  a
e  l  r  e  n  u  b  a  n  c  o  a
r  i  r  e  i  f  h  n  r  e  e  i
```

(quarter)   comprar   billetes   recibo
penny   dime   cambio   cochinito
dinero   nickel   banco   tienda

Word Find

Can you find the hidden words?
One word has been circled for you.
Find the other words.

```
b  u  y  b  i  l  l  n  f  d  d  i  s  m
i  a  c  b  a  n  k  i  s  p  e  n  d  m
m  c  a  s  h  o  d  c  f  d  f  e  o  v
o  l  c  e  o  o  y  k  d  o  l  l  a  r
n  c  s  l  e  r  u  e  e  y  s  c  e  e
e  r  o  l  e  o  s  l  r  d  e  b  i  t
y  e  l  r  p  o  n  q  a  a  n  d  c  r
a  d  d  e  r  n  u  o  i  e  l  h  c
e  i  o  c  i  a  h  a  c  o  s  t  a  h
t  t  c  e  c  i  e  r  t  e  o  t  n  r
y  o  h  i  e  i  s  t  s  r  e  c  g  t
c  h  e  p  e  f  e  a  n  t  e  e  e
l  t  c  t  d  a  o  r  n  p  e  n  n  y
f  e  k  s  a  l  d  i  m  e  i  e  n  e
```

(quarter)   spend   cash   bank   debit
penny   dime   bill   change money
credit   cost   price   sell   dollar
sold   buy   check   receipt

Answer Key

Pages 34–35
Students should circle 7 pennies.

Pages 36–37
Students should circle 9 dimes.

Page 38
1. Drawings will vary. 2. Students should circle *cobre*. 3. Drawings will vary.

Page 39
1. Drawings will vary. 2. Students should circle *copper*. 3. Drawings will vary.

Page 40
1. Students should circle *presidente*.
2. 10, 3. Students should circle ONE, ONE, OF, OF, OF, of, and of. 4. 9

Page 41
1. Students should circle *president*.
2. 10, 3. Students should circle ONE, ONE, OF, OF, OF, of, and of. 4. 9

Pages 42–43
1. 5, 2. 1, 3. 2 (including eagle's eye), 4. 1, 5. 31, 6. 9

Pages 44–45
1. $0.45, 2 nickels
2. $0.18, 3 pennies
3. $0.41, 4 dimes
4. $0.41, 1 quarter
5. $1.16, 1 dollar

Pages 46–47
from left to right then top to bottom: $6.00, $21.00, $20.00, $25.00, $10.00, $30.00, $40.00, $15.00, $2.00

Pages 48–49
from left to right then top to bottom: $42.00, $17.00, $16.00, $36.00, $61.00, $20.00

Pages 50–51
from left to right then top to bottom: $46.00, $300.00, $107.00, $40.00, $75.00, $55.00

Pages 52–53
from left to right then top to bottom: 50¢, 5¢, 2¢, 26¢, 6¢, 35¢, 30¢, 15¢, 11¢

Pages 54–55
from left to right then top to bottom: 41¢, 75¢, 38¢, 62¢, 80¢, 13¢, 18¢, 36¢, 32¢

Page 56
1. $1.95, 5¢, caramelo
2. Lisa, $0.45, 1
3. sí, sí, $2.35

Page 57
1. $1.95, 5¢, candy
2. Lisa, $0.45, 1
3. yes, yes, $2.35

Answer Key

Page 58
1. 3, 10¢
2. tomate
3. $1.50
4. no
5. $0.50
6. $0.80
7. 3
8. $1.80
9. 2, 10¢
10. $2.20

Page 59
1. 3, 10¢
2. tomato
3. $1.50
4. no
5. $0.50
6. $0.80
7. 3
8. $1.80
9. 2, 10¢
10. $2.20

Page 60
dime, cochinito, nickel, dólar, penny, monedas

Page 61
dime, bank, nickel, dollar, penny, coins

Page 62
quarter, cheque, dinero, recibo, cambio, precio

Page 63
quarter, check, money receipt, change, price

Pages 64–65
from left to right then top to bottom: 25¢, 35¢, 11¢, 30¢, 50¢, 26¢, 15¢, 2¢, 6¢, 15¢, 20¢, 10¢

Pages 66–67
from left to right then top to bottom: 61¢, 46¢, 36¢, 61¢, 45¢, 28¢, 52¢, 51¢

Pages 68–69

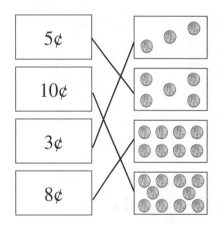

Pages 70–71

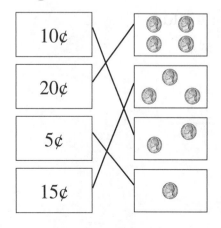

Answer Key

Pages 72–73

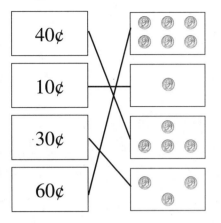

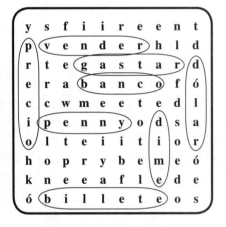

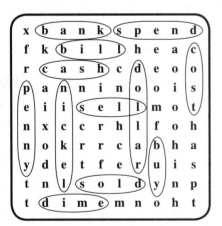

Page 74

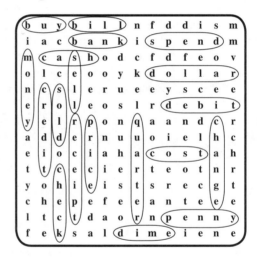

Page 74 word search:

```
y s f i i r e e n t
p v e n d e r h l d
r t e g a s t a r d
e r a b a n c o f ó
c c w m e e t e d l
i p e n n y o d s a
o l t e i i t i o r
h o p r y b e m e ó
k n e e a f l e d e
ó b i l l e t e o s
```

Page 75

```
x b a n k s p e n d
f k b i l l h e a c
r c a s h c d e o o
p a n n i n o o i s
e i i s e l l m o t
n x c c r h l f o h
n o k r r c a b h a
y d e t f e r u i s
t n l s o l d y n p
t d i m e m n o h t
```

Page 76

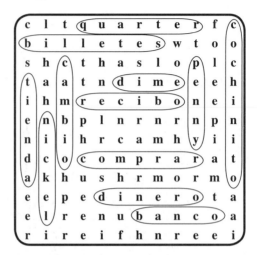

```
c l t q u a r t e r f c
b i l l e t e s w t o o
s h c t h a s l o p l c
t a a t n d i m e e e h
i h m r e c i b o n e i
e n b p l n r n r n p n
n i i h r c a m h y i p
d c o c o m p r a r a t
a k h u s h r m o r m o
e e p e d i n e r o t a
e l r e n u b a n c o a
r i r e i f h n r e e i
```

Page 77

```
b u y b i l l n f d d i s m
i a c b a n k i s p e n d m
m c a s h o d c f d f e o v
o l c e o o y k d o l l a r
n c s l e r u e e y s c e e
e r o l e o s l r d e b i t
y d l r p o n q a a n d c r
a d i e r n u u o i e l h c
e i o c i a h a c o s t h h
t t c e c i e r t e o t n r
y o h i e i s t s r e c g t
c h e p e f e e a n t e e e
l t c t d a o r n p e n n y
f e k s a l d i m e i e n e
```